CONTROL THE DAY

Powerful daily prayers that take charge of the day

31 daily devotional confessions to guide and inspire you each day

OLUWATOSIN OGIDAN

TABLE OF CONTENT

iii

ACKNOWLEDGMENTS

My deepest appreciation to……

The Lord Almighty, without whom writing this book would have been an impossible task.

Dr. Olusola Coker. I value your constant encouragement and the editorial skills you brought to bear in the making of this book.

Oluwafemi Ehindero, thanks for the great push, to make sure this book becomes a reality and for helping me to be the best version of myself.

Tolulope Ogidan, Toyosi Ogidan, Temitayo Ogidan, Michael Ogunremi, your constant support; and suggestions were quite useful and are highly appreciated.

Thanks to everyone that gave one advice or another, you; all did a wonderful job.

DEDICATION

For about 30 years, she was my closest friend, my prayer partner, my backbone, and constant support…..

Without her prayers, her love, and her support, this book might never have been written.

I dedicate this book to my lovely mother, Olabisi Ogidan.

And to all the great women who have struggled to achieve in one endeavor or the other.

Indeed, you will achieve it.

INTRODUCTION

Control the Day is a daily prayer to protect, guide, and inspire you for the day's activity. This book will help you seek the face of God each day of the month. It will inspire you to know what God has in stock for you on daily basis. Every prayer and confessions in each day will enable you to enjoy the favor each day has to offer. It will help you understand God's plan and grant you divine direction every single day of the month. You will be able to focus your time and attention on seeking God's plan for each day of every month. This book is valuable for those that need peace, encouragement, strength, protection, success, breakthrough, healing, miracle, etc for each day. You will discover reasons you need to control your day and the benefits attached to it.

This book is written to empower you scriptures and powerful prophetic declarations to take control of your day. As you meditate on these scriptures and make these declarations, expect God's power to rule your day. As the scripture says,

Psalm 68:19 Blessed be the Lord, who daily loadeth us with benefits, even the God of our salvation.

Words have spiritual powers that have the force to create physical manifestations.

The powerful daily confession written in this book should be confessed daily alongside the powerful prayer declaration for the day and you will see the massive daily results.

Testimonies of Overflowing Breakthrough shall be your portion in Jesus' name.

DAY ONE

Scriptural Meditation:

Psalms: 138:8: The LORD will perfect that which concerneth me: thy mercy, O LORD, endureth for ever: forsake not the works of thine own hands.

Philippians: 4:19: But my God shall supply all your need according to his riches in glory by Christ Jesus.

James: 1:17: Every good gift and every perfect gift is from above, and cometh down from the Father of lights, with whom is no variableness, neither shadow of turning.

Powerful Prayer Declaration:

As I step out today, let the heavens open for me, let the Glory of God fall upon my entire life. May the Lord grant me victory over every satanic device, let my root receive fire, and let the Holy

Spirit fill me afresh. Lord, today, break down every evil foundation of my life and rebuild a new one on Christ the Rock, cause your anointing to release fresh favor upon my life and let me enjoy the satisfaction of divine favor. As from this day, let the secret of my life be too hot for any foul spirit to handle. Let the power of darkness deleting the archive of my dream, collide with the Rock of Ages and let the vehicle of my dream, receive divine acceleration. I pray the grace of God, mercy, and favor of God, stand for me and my family in every area of life, in the Mighty Name of Jesus Christ, AMEN.

Prayer points for the day

- ➢ Prayer of Thanksgiving.
- ➢ Prayer of Forgiveness.
- ➢ Lord, remember your covenant of mercy with blessing upon my life.

- ➢ Father, honor my life with uncommon favor today.
- ➢ Father, remember your promises and turn things around for my good.

DAY TWO

Scriptural Meditations:

Isaiah: 41:13: For I the LORD thy God will hold thy right hand, saying unto thee, Fear not; I will help thee.

3John:1:2: Beloved, I wish above all things that thou mayest prosper and be in health, even as thy soul prospereth.

Powerful Prayer Declaration:

Today, I will not go backward but experience a breakthrough in all I do, all my requests shall be granted, I will continue to rejoice in God's presence. The grace of God will release the dew of heaven upon my life in Jesus' mighty name. I pray for this new day that the Lord Almighty God will manifest His Glorious power in my situation and make me a point of reference, a channel of blessings, a symbol of success, a vessel of testimonies, and a pillar of joy in Jesus name. Heaven will open for my sake and every blessing from above will locate me. Whatever I say or do shall be seasoned with favor. God's presence shall be my abode. Every power set to crumble my way and that of my household shall be shattered. God will attend to my situation this month and always in Jesus Wonderful name. Amen.

Prayer points for the day

- ➢ Prayer of Thanksgiving
- ➢ Prayer of Forgiveness
- ➢ Lord, let me not be replaced where I ought to be highly placed.
- ➢ Lord, let all my stolen blessings be restored in multiple folds.
- ➢ Lord, let blessings and peace be at my doorstep today and beyond in Jesus' name.
- ➢ I decree today, my land will not fail to bear fruit; I will be fruitful in all my endeavors.

DAY THREE

Scriptural Meditations:

Psalms: 61:3: For thou hast been a shelter for me, and a strong tower from the enemy.

Psalms: 124:7: Our soul is escaped as a bird out of the snare of the fowlers: the snare is broken, and we are escaped.

John: 1:16: And of his fulness have all we received, and grace for grace.

Exodus: 23:22: But if thou shalt indeed obey his voice, and do all that I speak; then I will be an enemy unto thine enemies, and an adversary unto thine` adversaries.

Powerful Prayer Declaration

Almighty Father, take me to the next level of expansion today and grant me the power to be fulfilled in life. Lord, in your mercy, show me the secret of my life and never give up on me. My God, transform my life and let every spirit of deception, working against me and my family be destroyed. As from this day, I shall find everlasting joy, for the Lion of the tribe of Judah, will turn the deceit and craftiness of the wicked into the stepping stones for my success. God, will not forsake me in the wilderness of life that I am in, but the Lord will send divine helpers that will make my dreams come true. Jehovah God, you will continually be my shield, fortress, and buckler, and in all these challenges of life, I shall come out better, stronger, greater, and richer. Every battle that is going on within and outside my heart, hear the voice of the Lord now, bow, and be still by the power in the blood of Jesus Christ, in the Mighty Name of Jesus Christ our Lord and Savior, Amen.

Prayer points for the day

➢ Sing Praises to the Almighty God.

- Ask God to forgive every known and unknown sin.

- This morning I pray in the matchless name of Jesus Christ, I am free from poverty, sickness, sorrow, fear, loneliness, debts, generational curse, demonic covenant, prayerlessness, and spiritual dryness, I am free from sin and nothing shall hold me down from rising in Jesus' name.

- Lord God, I will not be a victim of human error in the name of Jesus.

- Father, remove every shame and disappointments and replace them with Glory and divine appointments in Jesus' name.

DAY FOUR

Scriptural Meditations:

Deuteronomy:28:1-14: And it shall come to pass, if thou shalt hearken diligently unto the voice of the LORD thy God, to observe and to do all his commandments which I command thee this day, that the LORD thy God will set thee on high above all nations of the earth:

And all these blessings shall come on thee, and overtake thee, if thou shalt hearken unto the voice of the LORD thy God.

Blessed shalt thou be in the city, and blessed shalt thou be in the field.

Blessed shall be the fruit of thy body, and the fruit of thy ground, and the fruit of thy cattle, the increase of thy kine, and the flocks of thy sheep.

Blessed shall be thy basket and thy store.

Blessed shalt thou be when thou comest in, and blessed shalt thou be when thou goest out.

The LORD shall cause thine enemies that rise up against thee to be smitten before thy face: they shall come out against thee one way, and flee before thee seven ways.

The LORD shall command the blessing upon thee in thy storehouses, and in all that thou settest thine hand unto; and he shall bless thee in the land which the LORD thy God giveth thee.

The LORD shall establish thee and holy people unto himself, as he hath sworn unto thee, if thou shalt keep the commandments of the LORD thy God, and walk in his ways.

And all people of the earth shall see that thou art called by the name of the LORD; and they shall be afraid of thee.

And the LORD shall make thee plenteous in goods, in the fruit of thy body, and in the fruit of thy cattle, and in the fruit of thy ground, in the land which the LORD sware unto thy fathers to give thee.

The LORD shall open unto thee his good treasure, the heaven to give the rain unto thy land in his season, and to bless all the work of thine hand: and thou shalt lend unto many nations, and thou shalt not borrow.

And the LORD shall make thee the head, and not the tail; and thou shalt be above only, and thou shalt not be beneath; if that thou hearken unto the commandments of the LORD thy God, which I command thee this day, to observe and to do them:

And thou shalt not go aside from any of the words which I command thee this day, to the right hand, or to the left, to go after other gods to serve them.

Powerful Prayer Declaration:

I pray that this new day shall be a day of unlimited harvest, on this blessed day and beyond I declare that every good chapter closed by men against me shall be re-opened in my favor, those who gather to frustrate my vision shall beg to be part of my celebration. The Lord God shall give me a new name and identity, which will bury all the ugly stories associated with my background. The amazing grace of God that made Jabez more honorable than his brethren shall distinguish me amongst men. All areas where money may disgrace me, the mercy of God shall raise men of influence in my favor in Jesus mighty name. Those that conspired against Daniel and the three Hebrew men, paid with their lives, as I go out today, in the remaining days in this year and beyond whosoever desire to bring me down will receive God's anger without mercy and my Glory will manifest.

I will continue to enjoy the Goodness of the highest God and I will always stay lifted. It is my season of unlimited harvest in all areas of my life, the testimonies that my heart desire, Almighty God will give to me and my household in Jesus mighty name. AMEN.

Prayer points for the day

- ➤ Prayer of Thanksgiving.
- ➤ Prayer of Forgiveness.
- ➤ Oh Lord, on this glorious day, let the Heaven open for my sake and pour down your blessings upon me today.
- ➤ Father, let whatever I say or do today be seasoned with favor and let every blessing from above locate me.

➢ My Father, continue to strengthen and prosper me in all ways.

DAY FIVE

Scriptural Meditations:

2Samuel:9:7: And David said unto him, Fear not: for I will surely shew thee kindness for Jonathan thy father's sake, and will restore thee all the land of Saul thy father; and thou shalt eat bread at my table continually.

Exodus: 15:26: And said, If thou wilt diligently hearken to the voice of the LORD thy God, and wilt do that which is right in his sight, and wilt give ear to his commandments, and keep all his statutes, I will put none of these diseases upon thee, which I have brought upon the Egyptians: for I am the LORD that healeth thee.

1Corinthians:2:9: But as it is written, Eye hath not seen, nor ear heard, neither have entered into the heart of man, the things which God hath prepared for them that love him.

Powerful Prayer Declaration:

Rivers do not struggle to flow, I will never struggle to excel because I deserve the best. My dreams will not die, my plans will not fail, my destiny will not be aborted, and the desires of my heart will be granted. No one goes to the river early in the morning and brings back dirty water. My life will be clean, calm, and clear like the early morning water. The Grace of God will support, sustain, and supply all my needs in accordance with the riches of His glory. The Almighty God will restore to me what the wicked people had forcefully taken away from me. The Almighty God will bless me in whatever I do, protect me wherever I go. I pray that any junction the enemies are waiting for me before I get there, the Lord of host will fight for me. He will make my hopes become a reality and help me in every difficulty that comes my way in Jesus' name. AMEN

Prayer Points for the Day

> ➢ Sing Praises to God for keeping you alive.

> ➢ Ask God for mercy of every sin committed knowingly and unknowingly.

> ➢ My God, beautify my life today, add color to all I do and let me uniquely stand out in Jesus' mighty name.

> ➢ Every powerful enemy working against my progress, Lord destroy them completely in Jesus mighty name.

> ➢ Every witchcraft power eating up the profit of my work, I destroy your works over my life in the name of Jesus.

DAY SIX

Scriptural Meditations:

Revelation: 1:18: I am he that liveth, and was dead; and, behold, I am alive for evermore, Amen; and have the keys of hell and of death.

Hebrews: 10:36: For ye have need of patience, that, after ye have done the will of God, ye might receive the promise.

Isaiah: 41:10: Fear thou not; for I am with thee: be not dismayed; for I am thy God: I will strengthen thee; yea, I will help thee; yea, I will uphold thee with the right hand of my righteousness.

Powerful prayer declaration

Because the Lord lives:

My Future is guaranteed.

I will overcome challenges of life.

No weapon fashioned against me and my family shall prosper.

Every tongue that rises against me in judgment shall be condemned.

Every power frustrating my effort shall be scattered.

Every shackle of untimely death hanging over my neck shall be cut off today.

 I will recover all my lost glory.

My destiny helpers will locate me this month.

Every power delaying my benefits shall be destroyed by fire.

Those waiting to mock me shall be put to shame.

My hope is restored in Jesus Christ.

I will not be disappointed.

I will not experience sorrow and shame.

Sickness, calamity will not come near me and my household.

All my weeping shall turn to Joy.

I will fulfill destiny.

My years of disappointment, failure shall turn to testimony.

Every power aborting good things in my life becomes dead today in Jesus' name.

I am divinely favored.

I will be called upon for an appointment I did not deserve or labored for before the end of this month.

I will live the rest of my days on earth in peace and good health.

My generation will flourish like a Palm tree.

All these prophecies shall come to pass in my life today in the name of God the Father, Son, and the Holy Spirit, in Jesus mighty name Amen. My testimony will be seen, heard by many people in Jesus' name. AMEN.

Prayer Points for the Day

> Prayer of Thanksgiving.

> Prayer of Forgiveness.

> I pray today that the Lord will arise as Jehovah, God of war, and defend the lifting/progress/enthronement of me and my family members in the mighty name of Jesus.

> This day I will not suffer any breakdown, stagnation, frustration, depression, oppression, failure, loss, or untimely death in the name of Jesus.

> Every day God shall load me with benefits in the name of Jesus.

DAY SEVEN

Scriptural Meditations:

Isaiah: 40:31: But they that wait upon the LORD shall renew their strength; they shall mount up with wings as eagles; they shall run, and not be weary; and they shall walk, and not faint.

2Peter:1:2-4: Grace and peace be multiplied unto you through the knowledge of God, and of Jesus our Lord,

According as his divine power hath given unto us all things that pertain unto life and godliness, through the knowledge of him that hath called us to glory and virtue:

Whereby are given unto us exceeding great and precious promises: that by these ye might be partakers of the divine nature, having escaped the corruption that is in the world through lust.

Powerful Prayer Declaration

I decree and declare that;

The Lord will stand still for my case today in Jesus' name.

The Lord will respond to my cry today in Jesus' name.

My case will receive divine attention this day in Jesus' name.

The Lord will command his blessings upon my life today in Jesus' name.

The Lord will command his healing today in Jesus' name.

Those that have despised me shall come to honor me this season in Jesus' name.

The same mouth that has ridiculed me shall praise me this week in Jesus name.

The Lord will remove every garment of shame from my life in Jesus name.

The Lord will remove every garment of poverty from my life in Jesus name.

The Lord will terminate every garment of ridicule in my life in Jesus name.

Every demonic garment covering my glory shall catch fire in Jesus name.

Every obstacle on my way to glory shall be removed by fire in Jesus name.

Prayer Points for the Day

- Prayer of Thanksgiving.
- Prayer of Forgiveness.
- In the name of Jesus, my head will not be bowed in shame, reproach, and sorrow.

➢ Every attempt of the adversary to cause me pain and sorrow will fail woefully in the mighty name of Jesus.

➢ Plagues and noisome pestilence shall not come near my dwelling in the name of Jesus.

DAY EIGHT

Scriptural Meditations:

Matthew:6:30: Wherefore, if God so clothe the grass of the field, which today is, and tomorrow is cast into the oven, shall he not much more clothe you, O ye of little faith?

Therefore take no thought, saying, What shall we eat? or, What shall we drink? or, Wherewithal shall we be clothed?

(For after all these things do the Gentiles seek:) for your heavenly Father knoweth that ye have need of all these things.

But seek ye first the kingdom of God, and his righteousness; and all these things shall be added unto you.

Ephesians: 3:20: Now unto him that is able to do exceeding abundantly above all that we ask or think, according to the power that worketh in us,

Powerful Prayer Declaration

By the Mercies of the Almighty God, the Covenant Keeper, blessings shall follow and overtake me and my household today and always. Because the Sun will never ask for permission before shinning on nations, I will never bow my knees for anyone before I eat again in life in the Mighty Name of Jesus. Because the rain will never come down hot, my comfort in every area of life begins today in the Mighty Name of Jesus. Even as no one can count the Stars and number them, my wealth on earth will never be counted by anyone, and by the power that has been given to the Moon to displays its beauty and illumination in the dark, I will forever shine in the midst of the people that don't even want to hear anything about me for good in life and they shall not be able to harm me in the Mighty Name of Jesus.

Prayer Points for the Day

- ➤ Prayer of Thanksgiving.
- ➤ Prayer of Forgiveness.
- ➤ Father, let every plan of the enemy to afflict my finances be wasted in the name of Jesus.
- ➤ Father, let my efforts and labor throughout today by your divine help yield bountiful results in Jesus' name.
- ➤ Father, let my going out and coming in be blessed in the name of Jesus.
- ➤ Father, let your peace dwell richly with me and my family throughout today in Jesus' name.

DAY NINE

Scriptural Meditations:

Job: 36:11: If they obey and serve him, they shall spend their days in prosperity, and their years in pleasures.

Jude: 1:24: Now unto him that is able to keep you from falling, and to present you faultless before the presence of his glory with exceeding joy,

Isaiah: 58:8: Then shall thy light break forth as the morning, and thine health shall spring forth speedily: and thy righteousness shall go before thee; the glory of the LORD shall be thy rereward.

Powerful Prayer Declaration

I give thanks to God for this day in which my dreams will flourish, my plans will succeed, my destiny will be assured, and the desire of my heart will be granted in Jesus name. The breakthrough I need will know my name and address, before the end of today. As I awake this morning, may my life be as clean, calm, and clear as the early morning dew. May the grace of the Almighty support, sustain and supply all my needs according to His riches in my life, there is no more famine but a total blessing, no more lack but abundance, no more debt but riches, no more delay but progress. My enemies shall fail and fall. My pains shall end, my gains shall take over. The LORD will visit me and there shall be showers of blessings upon my life in the Mighty Name of Jesus Christ. I shall be blessed, I shall be celebrated and people shall attest to the goodness of God in my life. Everything around me and all that I come across will always be in my favor. I will not be overwhelmed by the uncertainty of life, God's benevolence will always stand me out, in the mighty name of Jesus Christ.

Prayer Points for the Day

- ➢ Prayer of thanksgiving.

- ➢ Prayer of forgiveness.

- ➢ There is no door that mercy of God cannot open, it opened Bartholomew's blind eyes, opened Elizabeth's barren womb, opened the Red sea for the Israelites, and terminated 430years of slavery, Father, open the door of Mercy unto me today.

- ➢ As I rise up this morning, Angels of help and Mercy rise up and work for me in Jesus' name.

- ➢ Father, let every good door shut against me be opened in the Mighty name of Jesus.

- ➢ Father, open the door of blessings, Joy, Happiness, Prosperity, Salvation, and every good thing unto me today.

DAY TEN

Scriptural Meditations:

Psalms: 1:3: And he shall be like a tree planted by the rivers of water, that bringeth forth his fruit in his season; his leaf also shall not wither; and whatsoever he doeth shall prosper.

Genesis: 1:28: And God blessed them, and God said unto them, Be fruitful, and multiply, and replenish the earth, and subdue it: and have dominion over the fish of the sea, and over the fowl of the air, and over every living thing that moveth upon the earth.

2Corinthians:9:8: And God is able to make all grace abound toward you; that ye, always having all sufficiency in all things, may abound to every good work:

(As it is written, He hath dispersed abroad; he hath given to the poor: his righteousness remaineth for ever.

Now he that ministereth seed to the sower both minister bread for your food, and multiply your seed sown, and increase the fruits of your righteousness;)

Powerful Prayer Declaration

 Sovereign Lord, be my coach today and let your angels defend me when I get attacked by the enemy's strike so that I will be able to achieve and keep my goals. Let great people support my dreams and help me never to give up on my dreams until I achieve them. I will score high on my visions and God will make me a winner. I will do well in life and will never go on reverse; nothing will cause me to break down. As I accelerate, I will overtake those in front of me and as I drive my goals, there will be no disaster. I will never be diagnosed with a terminal illness. If there is any hidden sickness in your body, I proclaim the blood of Jesus to put it on treatment, every day I will be checked up by the angels of God and they will give me the necessary prescriptions to follow my pursuit of success. I decree loud divine presence, mercy, and uncommon favor into my profession/ career or handiwork this new day in Jesus' name. Fruitfulness in every area of my life is my portion this day in this month of harvest in Jesus' name. In whatsoever I lay my hand doing, I shall surely prosper. Wherever I find myself this week, I will record unimaginable success in Jesus' name. At the end of this week, I will definitely have a cause to testify and sing Hallelujah choruses in Jesus' name.

Prayer Points for the Day

- ➢ Sing Praises to the Almighty God.

- ➢ Ask for Mercy for known and unknown sins.

- ➢ Lord God, let me experience supernatural expansion on all fronts in the light of your Glory and Grace in Jesus' Name.

- ➢ Father Lord, let me continually eat the good of the land.

- ➢ Father Lord, make me fruitful in my daily work both in and out of season.

DAY ELEVEN

Scriptural Meditations:

1John:4:4: Ye are of God, little children, and have overcome them: because greater is he that is in you, than he that is in the world.

Romans: 15:29: And I am sure that, when I come unto you, I shall come in the fullness of the blessing of the gospel of Christ.

Powerful Prayer Declaration

Let the heavens open, and let the glory of God fall upon me today. May the Lord, grant me victory over every satanic device and let my root receive fire and let the Holy Spirit fill me afresh. May the Lord, break down every evil foundation of my life today; rebuild a new one on Christ the Rock. May the Lord, cause His anointing to release fresh favor upon my life and let me enjoy the satisfaction of divine favor. As from this day, let the secret of my life; be too hot for any foul spirit to handle. From the East, West, South and North, God's favor and honor will find me. The Holy Spirit that is at work in me will do exceedingly and abundantly more than I can ever think or ask in JESUS Name, Amen. I have abundance in all things, and I receive the release of a bountiful harvest, a thousand-fold increase, the opening of the storehouses in heaven, wealth on earth, and eternity with God, in JESUS Name Amen.

Prayer Points for the Day

- Prayer of Thanksgiving
- Prayer of forgiveness
- Father Lord, let every dry area in my life receive the release of the dew of heaven.
- Father, let there be abundant rain, the latter and the former together.
- In the Name of JESUS, I will see an increase all around this day. Amen

DAY TWELVE

Scriptural Meditations:

Joel 2:27: And ye shall know that I am in the midst of Israel, that I am the LORD your God, and none else: and my people shall never be ashamed.

Isaiah: 41:17: When the poor and needy seek water, and there is none, and their tongue faileth for thirst, I the LORD will hear them, I the God of Israel will not forsake them.

Isaiah: 44:3: For I will pour water upon him that is thirsty, and floods upon the dry ground: I will pour my spirit upon thy seed, and my blessing upon thine offspring

Powerful Prayer Declaration

I decree and declare that;

The Lord will show Himself mighty for me this day in Jesus' name.

The Lord will prove Himself in my life as the mighty restorer this day in Jesus' name.

The Lord will divinely intervene in my life this day in Jesus' name.

The Lord will prove to all my mockers this day that He is God in Jesus' name.

The Lord will terminate every shame and reproach in my life in Jesus' name.

The Lord will deliver me from every form of embarrassment this day in Jesus' name.

God will arrest every arrester of my destiny in Jesus' name.

Every root of shame in my life is uprooted today in Jesus' name.

Every object of shame in my life shall be turned to an object of glory in Jesus' name.

The favor of God shall answer for my total recovery this day in Jesus' name.

Prayer Points for the Day

- ➢ Prayer of Thanksgiving.
- ➢ Prayer of Forgiveness.
- ➢ Father Lord, be glorified in my life.
- ➢ Father Lord, everywhere the soles of my feet shall walk, let it be given to me as an inheritance.
- ➢ Father Lord, let me walk freely continually in the place of honor in JESUS Name Amen.

DAY THIRTEEN

Scriptural Meditations:

1 Thessalonians: 5:24: Faithful is he that calleth you, who also will do it.

Habakkuk 3:19: The LORD God is my strength, and he will make my feet like hinds' feet, and he will make me to walk upon mine high places.

Powerful Prayer Declaration

Oh Lord, my God provide and meet me at every point of need. I have waited enough; the change I expect is upon me, God exceeds my expectations. The chains of delay are broken and every covering of darkness over my tomorrow is rolled away in JESUS Name Amen. I receive the oil of ease, the anointing that makes all goals and divine accomplishments easy. God's favor is in me, and the earth shall yield her increase for me. Strangers shall serve me, and men shall serve me. Greatness is my portion, in Jesus' name. As the mountain surrounds Jerusalem, so the Lord encamps around me. His presence will be my guide. Lord, grant me a new beginning and I will stand out and not fail in JESUS Name. As the clouds stand without pillars; as oceans move without engines, and rain falls without a pump, so shall my blessings be unsearchable! The Lord shall make me a delight to my generation in JESUS Name Amen.

Prayer Points for the Day

> ➢ Prayer of Thanksgiving.

> ➢ Prayer of Forgiveness.

> ➢ Father Lord, every altar erected against me knowingly or unknowingly that is not in line with your will pull them down today.

> ➢ Father Lord, renew my strength and make my life blossom.

> ➢ Father Lord, let me walk in your grace today in the name of Jesus.

➢ Father, let this be my season of restoration and refreshing in JESUS Name Amen.

DAY FOURTEEN

Scriptural Meditations:

Psalms: 94:17: Unless the LORD had been my help, my soul had almost dwelt in silence.

Psalms: 81:10: I am the LORD thy God, which brought thee out of the land of Egypt: open thy mouth wide, and I will fill it.

Powerful Prayer Declaration

I am ready to rise today. When that storm is over, I am not going to be defeated. I am going to rise up healthy, blessed, and prosperous. I am not going to look like what I have been through. My enemies are paying for what they brought me through. I am divinely helped and heavenly assisted. I live in the sufficient and amazing grace of God. I am a recipient of God's mercy. I will experience God's goodness afresh in JESUS Name. God shall bless me and all the ends of the earth shall fear Him. Then shall the earth yield her increase; and God, even our God shall bless me and my household. God is eternally committed to me. I am the recipient of His faithfulness; no carefully designed conspiracy of hell against my God-ordained destiny shall stand. I dwell in the land and feed on His faithfulness in JESUS Name. The word of God works for me. Heaven is opened to me, and God helps me. The earth supports me, and I will continually live by His sufficient and amazing grace in JESUS Name, Amen.

Prayer Points for the Day

> Prayer of Thanksgiving.

> Prayer of Forgiveness.

> The Ancient of days, set me on the right path of excellence today.

> Sovereign Lord, work things out for my good today.

- ➢ Oh Lord, My God, bless me indeed and enlarge my coast.

DAY FIFTEEN

Scriptural Meditations

Psalms: 37:25: I have been young, and now am old; yet have I not seen the righteous forsaken, nor his seed begging bread.

He is ever merciful, and lendeth; and his seed is blessed.

Hebrews: 3:6: But Christ as a son over his own house; whose house are we, if we hold fast the confidence and the rejoicing of the hope firm unto the end.

Powerful Prayer Declaration

I am the zenith of God's creation and I will continually manifest His good works in CHRIST JESUS. I will see good and experience His grace because I am his image and likeness. God will see me through to the end and bring me into the new season of victory. His promises will yet overtake me. My life counts for the best because my tomorrow is sure in CHRIST JESUS. God is faithfully consistent and will never fail me. I will finish strong; His grace keeps me. Might and power from His presence make the difference in my life to the glory of His Name. God's thoughts of good and not of evil deliver to me a bright future; I have a living hope according to His divine plan. Everything works for my good for the purpose of His will in JESUS Name. I am set apart for God's tender mercies to be seen in your life. His life and light will continually shine through me. His faithfulness is lifting my head by Grace in JESUS Name.

Prayer Points for the Day

➢ Sing Praise to the God who has kept you alive.

➢ Ask for mercy; tell him to forgive every sin hindering you from getting your testimony.

➢ Father Lord, let your voice of thunders from heaven command an end to all seeming void and formlessness in my life.

➢ My Lord, My Father, let the Light of your countenance flood my path and let every chaotic condition in my life be reordered by your word in JESUS Name.

➢ Father, let me celebrated today in the mighty name of Jesus.

DAY SIXTEEN

Scriptural Meditations:

Philippians: 4:7: And the peace of God, which passeth all understanding, shall keep your hearts and minds through Christ Jesus.

Joel: 2:23: Be glad then, ye children of Zion, and rejoice in the LORD your God: for he hath given you the former rain moderately, and he will cause to come down for you the rain, the former rain, and the latter rain in the first month.

Powerful Prayer Declaration:

Sovereign God, let your plan unfolds in every area of my life as I yield to your Lordship. I am firmly established in your love and covered by your absolute power and grace. I know you have my back, and my tomorrow is secured in JESUS Name. Mercy finds me wherever I turn to. For shame, I receive a double portion of honor. For every battle in my life, I have been pronounced victorious; I break forth on every side in JESUS Name. By the blood of the eternal covenant, God remembers me for good. His blessing-bearing angels locate me, and He smiles upon me and rewards me bountifully this season in JESUS Name Amen. God has lifted my head and carried me over in the midst of troubled days and delivered me from every unpleasant event. My light shines always and the Glory of God upon me will not be covered in JESUS Name.

Prayer Points for the Day

> Prayer of Thanksgiving

> Prayer of forgiveness.

> Father Lord, deliver me from every evil plot set to destroy my destiny.

> Father Lord, every association of the enemy against me and my seed(s) will not stand in the name of Jesus.

> Oh Lord God, every conspiracy of the evil men in hidden places against me is shattered in JESUS Name Amen.

DAY SEVENTEEN

Scriptural Meditations:

Joel: 2:21: Fear not, O land; be glad and rejoice: for the LORD will do great things.

Proverb: 12:14: A man shall be satisfied with good by the fruit of his mouth: and the recompence of a man's hands shall be rendered unto him.

Powerful Prayer Declaration

God, My King, You are Lord and Father; I have an eternally enduring heritage in you. I am kept and jealously guarded as the apple of your eye. My life is precious to you. You give men up for my soul and watch over me. God cover me and put a fresh fragrance of favor upon me, clothe me with your glory. Kings and royalty shall honor and serve me, and the mighty in the land will entreat my favor in JESUS Name. I am completely protected and jealously guarded by God. He is lifting me above all forms of the conspiracy of evil men and distinguishes amongst others this season. The Lord wraps me with the garments of rejoicing, makes me laugh again, lifts me and causes me to find peace again. I am dazed by God's mercy and I exceed all limits set over me by men in JESUS Name. I am overshadowed by the light of God's glory and darkness cannot comprehend it in JESUS Name. God will nurture and stabilize me on higher ground and perfect everything that concerns me. Nothing can stop the flow of God's Grace in my life. My joy is full, for I am lifted to the place where I belong. I am upheld by the righteous right hand of The Lord Most High. My eyes are on you to keep me in safety. You are my banner of victory and the covering of my head in the days of battle in JESUS Name. Amen

Prayer Points for the Day

- ➢ Prayer of Thanksgiving.
- ➢ Prayer of Forgiveness.
- ➢ Father, please pour your salt into my source and change every curse into my life to a blessing.
- ➢ Father, speak to my body Lord, and everything that is damaged beyond repair, replace it.
- ➢ Father, please command an end to darkness in my life.

DAY EIGHTEEN

Scriptural Meditations:

Psalms: 18:44: As soon as they hear of me, they shall obey me: the strangers shall submit themselves unto me.

Proverb: 3:33: The curse of the LORD is in the house of the wicked: but he blesseth the habitation of the just.

Psalms: 103:3 -5: Who forgiveth all thine iniquities; who healeth all thy diseases;

Who redeemeth thy life from destruction; who crowneth thee with lovingkindness and tender mercies;

Who satisfieth thy mouth with good things; so that thy youth is renewed like the eagle's.

Powerful Prayer Declaration

Everything that tries to exalt itself above the name of God in my life is humiliated in the name of Jesus. I will be nourished in and out of season, like a tree planted by the riverside in JESUS Name. God defend, keep, and protect me, and do not allow me to be subverted in my course in JESUS Name. My Father, paralyze the influence of hell set against me, destroy the conspiracy of the envious and scatter the siege set by the wicked against me. The snare is broken, and my feet have escaped in JESUS Name. God shields me from trouble and terror. I am protected from the oppression of the enemy. Help arises for me out of Zion, and I will never suffer any form of injury in any area of my life in JESUS Name. Lord Jesus brighten my day with that which makes me shine, and let the light of my home, endeavors, and pursuit shine again, in Jesus mighty name. As I look up to the hills where my help comes from, may I see JESUS high, and lifted above each of my needs and may His presence make a lot of difference in my life in JESUS Name.

Prayer Points for the Day

- Prayer of Thanksgiving.
- Prayer of forgiveness.
- Father, rain your blessings on me today.
- Father, please wipe away tears from my eyes.
- Father, let every curse in my life be broken and reversed in Jesus' name.

DAY NINETEEN

Scriptural Meditations:

Colossians: 1:11: Strengthened with all might, according to his glorious power, unto all patience and longsuffering with joyfulness;

Philippians: 2:13: For it is God which worketh in you both to will and to do of his good pleasure.

Powerful Prayer Declaration:

The Lord has lifted my head and the light of His countenance shines over me. He has remembered me for good according to His promise, so all things are working together for my good in JESUS Name. The city gate opens to me, I prosper like never before; the Lord has announced my lifting. Good things overshadow you, and I am lifted indeed, in Jesus' name. Troubles from any quarter are averted because I bear on my body the marks of the Lord JESUS. I walk in grace amazingly and abundantly. I have the newness of life and walk in His love divine! It is well with me in JESUS Name. God will bring to pass in your life miracles I cannot number. He'll cause great and mighty things of joy that are beyond human understanding to continually happen in my life in JESUS Name. God will give me a latter rain for all times of dryness. He'll cause me to move with an unstoppable speed in JESUS Name. I am established over every plan and limitation of darkness and I am at liberty to find full expression in purpose in JESUS Name.

Prayer Points for the Day

 ➢ Sing praises to the Almighty God.

 ➢ Ask for forgiveness of every known and unknown sin.

 ➢ My God, take me out of every uncomfortable position and place me in a place of comfort, breakthrough, joy, peace and favor as I journey through life.

- ➢ Father, show up for me in all my endeavors.
- ➢ Father, let all my good efforts yield fruitful results in Jesus' name.

DAY TWENTY

Scriptural Meditations:

Romans: 15:13: Now the God of hope fill you with all joy and peace in believing, that ye may abound in hope, through the power of the Holy Ghost.

Joel: 2:26: And ye shall eat in plenty, and be satisfied, and praise the name of the LORD your God, that hath dealt wondrously with you: and my people shall never be ashamed

Powerful Prayer Declaration:

I excel above all challenges; I rule above all unpleasant decrees. My word is saturated by the power of God, through grace. Nothing can stop me because He's involved in my race in life, and I am an embodiment of grace in JESUS Name. By the power in the blood of the eternal covenant, every set up against me shall fall for my sake. All hurt targeted at me shall come to fruitlessness.

He who has the heart of the King in His hands and turns it wherever He pleases turn the hearts of kings and rulers in my favor. The peace of the Lord that passes all understanding garrisons my heart. LORD, lift me from the desert and dry places of life and place me on the throne prepared for me from the foundation of the earth. Grace and mercy sort me out in JESUS Name. My good labor will not be in vain.

Prayer Points for the Day

- Prayer of Thanksgiving.
- Prayer of Forgiveness.
- LORD God, hide me in the safety of your hidden place.
- My God, remember your covenant of mercy and paralyze every appearance of wickedness set up to trouble me in JESUS Name Amen.

➢ Every strongman of my father's house, my mother's house, and my in-law's house this very year shall submit themselves unto me in Jesus name.

DAY TWENTY-ONE

Scriptural Meditations:

Hosea: 14:5: I will be as the dew unto Israel: he shall grow as the lily, and cast forth his roots as Lebanon.

His branches shall spread, and his beauty shall be as the olive tree, and his smell as Lebanon.

They that dwell under his shadow shall return; they shall revive as the corn, and grow as the vine: the scent thereof shall be as the wine of Lebanon.

Ephraim shall say, What have I to do any more with idols? I have heard him, and observed him: I am like a green fir tree. From me is thy fruit found.

Psalms: 92:12: The righteous shall flourish like the palm tree: he shall grow like a cedar in Lebanon.

Those that be planted in the house of the LORD shall flourish in the courts of our God.

They shall still bring forth fruit in old age; they shall be fat and flourishing;

Powerful Prayer Declaration:

The power of God will destroy every seeming yoke, burden, and pressure upon my life. God, restore unto me the freshness of my blessed future. Let your joy continually strengthens me, and the dew of heaven break every hardness around me. Peace is restored unto me in JESUS name. I am empowered by God like never before to fulfill my destiny. The divine enablement to move into greater glory comes over me, and His power overshadows me to make everything that is said to be impossible a possibility for me in Jesus' name. My life is crowned with fatness, my mouth is filled with good things, life favors me and

God honors me. Things work for my good and I will shine forth in JESUS Name. The brightness of a thousand stars cannot stand the glory of a moon, so shall the glory of God in me be celebrated among millions. God will lay His fingers upon everything I touch today and wipe away all tears from my eyes. I am blessed with all spiritual blessings in heavenly places. I shall experience supernatural abundance from the Lord. God will fulfill His promises in my life and make me swim in the abundance of His blessings. So shall it be In Jesus mighty name.

Prayer of the Day

- ➤ Prayer of Thanksgiving
- ➤ Prayer of Forgiveness
- ➤ Lord God, settle each of my fears and heart cry this day and beyond.
- ➤ Lord God, let me enjoy peace like a river.

- ➢ Lord God, let sickness, disease, and death be far away from me and my household. Sound health shall be my lot.

DAY TWENTY-TWO

Scriptural Meditations:

Isaiah 45:2-3: I will go before thee, and make the crooked places straight: I will break in pieces the gates of brass, and cut in sunder the bars of iron

Genesis: 26:4: And I will make thy seed to multiply as the stars of heaven, and will give unto thy seed all these countries; and in thy seed shall all the nations of the earth be blessed;

Psalms: 133:1: Behold, how good and how pleasant it is for brethren to dwell together in unity!

It is like the precious ointment upon the head, that ran down upon the beard, even Aaron's beard: that went down to the skirts of his garments;

As the dew of Hermon, and as the dew that descended upon the mountains of Zion: for there the LORD commanded the blessing, even life for evermore.

Powerful Prayer Declaration

These are the days of my appointments. My waiting is significantly rewarded with anticipated changes in JESUS Name. I am a living hope, and I have a glorious future. My procession is triumphant. My tomorrow is better than today as I shine brighter and brighter unto a perfect day in JESUS Name.

God is at work in me both to will and to do of His good pleasure. As my eyes behold the brightness of the shining of His word; I do not walk in darkness but have the goodness of the light of His presence.

My light has come, and I am reborn into greatness as ordained by God. Things happen for me, and the lines have fallen for me in pleasant places in JESUS Name Amen.

God will lift my head and advance my course in life. Heaven declares a change in my season, and the proclamation of progress has been made in JESUS Name.

This day, rough situations shall be made straight for me, Tough circumstances shall be turned around for you my good. Firmly shut doors shall be opened for me, and I shall reap abundantly from the treasures and secret resources of God in Jesus' name. AMEN.

Prayer of the Day

- ➢ Prayer of thanksgiving.
- ➢ Prayer of forgiveness.

- ➢ Lord God, No weapon against me shall prosper in the name of Jesus.

- ➢ Lord God, sorrow and grief will not be my portion. Joy unspeakable shall be your testimony.

- ➢ Lord God, deliver me from every bondage, satanic oppression, and affliction.

DAY TWENTY-THREE

Scriptural Meditations:

Psalms: 41:2: The LORD will preserve him, and keep him alive; and he shall be blessed upon the earth: and thou wilt not deliver him unto the will of his enemies.

Zechariah10:1: Ask ye of the LORD rain in the time of the latter rain; so the LORD shall make bright clouds, and give them showers of rain, to everyone grass in the field.

Powerful Prayer Declaration

On this glorious day, I will increase in the revelation of God and He will take me to new heights in Him. His goodness and glory envelopes me and the dew from heaven refreshes me in JESUS name. God's blessing is upon me and my household beyond expectations today.

God's will is done in my life and His grace flows freely towards me. I am profiled for greatness; I am a city set on a hill. My light cannot be hidden, because I am a beacon of hope to all around me.

The Angel that brings good news shall locate me and my family and I shall have great joy. Heaven and earth shall rejoice with me in Jesus' Name. Amen.

My feet will not enter the place of destruction because God has not ordained for me the story of shame nor disgrace in Jesus Name. Amen.

The Presence of God be with me in all my ways today; May the Glory of God manifest in all my doings; I will experience Divine Assurance in all my endeavors, And may every moment be characterized by God's REST for me and all mine this day In Jesus' name. AMEN.

Prayer for the Day

- ➢ Prayer of Thanksgiving.

- ➢ Prayer of Forgiveness.

- ➢ Father, do not let me lack any good thing, let abundance and prosperity be my heritage.

- ➢ Father, let those who gather to frustrate my God-given vision beg to be part of my celebration.

- ➢ Father, let my tomorrow be alright, in the mighty name of JESUS.

DAY TWENTY-FOUR

Scriptural Meditations:

Isaiah: 45:8: Drop down, ye heavens, from above, and let the skies pour down righteousness: let the earth open, and let them bring forth salvation, and let righteousness spring up together; I the LORD have created it.

Isaiah: 60:1: Arise, shine; for thy light is come, and the glory of the LORD is risen upon thee.

Powerful Prayer Declaration

The Lord is crowning me and all my works with a bountiful harvest. Helpers are coming my way to do that which the Lord has sent them to do in my life and family.

As my desire reaches heaven, miracles are activated for me; because the Lord's hand is stretched out in grace and mercy to me in JESUS Name.

Anywhere I have been forgotten, Almighty God is opening a supernatural door of remembrance for me. That hidden tears in my inner heart is turning to greater testimonies. What is impossible for others around me shall be possible for me in JESUS Name.

In this time of my life, God by His Spirit unfolds and ushers me into another phase of greatness according to His eternal and sovereign plan where everything is commanded to work together for my good in JESUS Name.

I am set up for a sudden miracle because God approves and upholds my course. I will go forth to overcome and surmount any other mountain and challenges on my way today in the name of Jesus.

Prayer for the Day

- Prayer of Thanksgiving.

- Prayer of Forgiveness.

- In the name of Jesus, I decree any power waiting for me to weep, mourn or cry shall be suffocated.

- Every force assigned to choke my blessings, be crushed to pieces in the name of Jesus.

- Lord, there be the sound of abundance of rain upon my business.

DAY TWENTY-FIVE

Scriptural Meditations:

Philippians: 2:9: Wherefore God also hath highly exalted him, and given him a name which is above every name:

That at the name of Jesus every knee should bow, of things in heaven, and things in earth, and things under the earth;

And that every tongue should confess that Jesus Christ is Lord, to the glory of God the Father.

Psalms: 3:3: But thou, O LORD, art a shield for me; my glory, and the lifter up of mine head.

Powerful Prayer Declaration

On this glorious day, I will lie down in green pasture and enjoy the peace of God. God is moving on my behalf to reach out to me abundantly beyond my scope in JESUS Name Amen.

The glory of the Lord has risen upon me. I am shielded on all sides, protected, and guided by the host of angels. My life is aligned with the will of God, so I cannot stray or be stranded in JESUS Name.

The Shepherd of my soul is in full control of my living. He is my fortress. He is my God. He is my hope, I will make it, I will not fail, I will not fall, and I will fulfill my purpose, and exceed every expectation in JESUS name.

I am eternally relevant to God's scheme of things; my glory cannot be covered. The tops of my mountains are visible for all eyes to see. I will not be passed on by events. I will remain on the cutting edge in JESUS Name.

The voice of the Lord will stand out for me, no matter the noise around me; His word will speak for me no matter what the enemy is saying. He will help, keep, uphold, sustain, protect, defend and exalt me in the name of JESUS CHRIST.

God is magnified for His grace and wisdom given to me. Great things will be heard and said of me. His glory will do impossible things for me in JESUS Name.

Prayer for the Day

- ➢ Prayer of Thanksgiving.
- ➢ Prayer of Forgiveness.
- ➢ Lord God, please destroy every force working against my progress in Jesus' name.
- ➢ Holy Spirit, give me a teachable spirit.
- ➢ Lord Jesus, make me a blessing to my generation.

DAY TWENTY-SIX

Scriptural Meditations:

Ezekiel: 36:8: But ye, O mountains of Israel, ye shall shoot forth your branches, and yield your fruit to my people of Israel; for they are at hand to come.

For, behold, I am for you, and I will turn unto you, and ye shall be tilled and sown:

Revelation:21:11: Having the glory of God: and her light was like unto a stone most precious, even like a jasper stone, clear as crystal;

Powerful Prayer Declaration

The Almighty God by His divine intervention will cause the chapter of uncommon miracles in my life to be opened on this day.

God is working in my favor. He makes all things new for me. I am created for excellence and I will win always in JESUS Name.

I am a partaker of the divine nature. I am lifted, I go forward, and I increase on all sides. I am upheld by the righteous right hand of God. Grace is released to me in JESUS Name Amen.

Dry bones are revived, and God gives me the victory. He holds my hands and leads me with His eyes. The former things are passed, and He does a new thing in my life. Shame and disgrace are far from me. I am a person of honor, mercy, and grace in JESUS Name Amen.

I go from glory to glory and move from grace to grace. I increase in all I do, I see God's faithfulness in all I do, and I will see good all the days of my life in JESUS Name.

Prayer points for the Day

- Prayer of Thanksgiving.

- Prayer of Forgiveness.

- In the name of Jesus, I speak unstoppable advancement upon my life.

- Father, let my ears hear good news and let me walk in victory and liberty of the Holy Spirit every day in Jesus Mighty Name.

- Father, let your Mighty hand be upon my life, upholding and protecting me from all those who rise up against me in Jesus' name.

DAY TWENTY-SEVEN

Scriptural Meditations:

Exodus: 33:14, 18: And he said, My presence shall go with thee, and I will give thee rest.

And he said, I beseech thee, shew me thy glory.

Isaiah: 45:2: I will go before thee, and make the crooked places straight: I will break in pieces the gates of brass, and cut in sunder the bars of iron:

And I will give thee the treasures of darkness, and hidden riches of secret places, that thou mayest know that I, the LORD, which call thee by thy name, am the God of Israel.

Powerful Prayer Declaration:

God is my God forever, and He is my Guide from now till the end of time. I will not suffer any hurt; because He lives, my future is secured in JESUS Name.

I have a brighter tomorrow: I operate under open heavens and backed by the heavenly host, and the throne of God gives me support. I overcome the world and all that is in it in JESUS Name Amen.

God who rules and reigns in Heaven and on earth will show up for me and I will experience the manifestation of His will and the fulfillment of His precious promises in JESUS Name.

I AM the apple of God's eye and He guards me jealously. No evil shall come near me, no pestilence shall invade my dwelling, and I am delivered from every plague and protected from every ill wind in JESUS Name.

If God could save me from Death, Satan and Hell, there's nothing else He can't save me from. His grace overflows on my behalf. His Blessings are on me in JESUS Name Amen.

Prayer of the Day

- Sing praises to the Lord of Host.

- Ask for Mercy of every Known and unknown sin.

- Father Lord, break me free from every average mindset.

- Father, grant me the spirit of excellence.

- Oh Lord, increase my productivity in my daily activities.

DAY TWENTY-EIGHT

Scriptural Meditations:

Jeremiah: 29:10: For thus saith the LORD, That after seventy years be accomplished at Babylon I will visit you, and perform my good word toward you, in causing you to return to this place.

Isaiah: 41:10: Fear thou not; for I am with thee: be not dismayed; for I am thy God: I will strengthen thee; yea, I will help thee; yea, I will uphold thee with the right hand of my righteousness.

Powerful Prayer Declaration

Heaven will speak for me as God's candidate. His peace and grace will be evident in me. The river of His righteousness flows over me and brings forth a shout of joy in JESUS Name.

Jesus bore all my infirmities in His own body; therefore, I refuse to be brought down by sickness. In Him, I live in divine health. The Name of Jesus has been named upon me, and daily, I enjoy the impact of God's divine presence in my life! I declare that my physical body is vitalized by the power of God's Spirit, and it is shielded and protected from all evil, in Jesus' Name.

The Heavens have poured out the rain on my field. The good work of my hands is blessed and I harvest in abundance in JESUS Name Amen.

I manifest the good and great grace of the Lord. I go forward in life and promotion comes my way on all sides, as I enter into the season of laughter and unceasing increase in JESUS Name.

God favor my cause, and nothing can hold me back. I rise on eagles' wings; I activate the pleasures of His presence and yoke of pressure is destroyed in JESUS Name.

The loving-kindness of the Lord blows pleasantness on my path from every wing of the wind. I prosper as God has commanded. I am in health as He has declared. I have peace as He has provided, His blood covers me as expected, and I have dominion in JESUS Name Amen.

Prayer for the Day

- ➢ Prayer of Thanksgiving.
- ➢ Prayer of Forgiveness.
- ➢ Father, let every rough situation in my life be made straight in the name of Jesus.
- ➢ Father, let every tough situation operating in my destiny be turned for my good in the Mighty name of Jesus.
- ➢ Father, let every firmly shut door of breakthrough be opened and let me reap abundantly from your treasures and secret resources in the mighty name of Jesus.

DAY TWENTY-NINE

Scriptural Meditations:

Psalms: 20:1: The LORD hear thee in the day of trouble; the name of the God of Jacob defend thee;

Send thee help from the sanctuary, and strengthen thee out of Zion;

Remember all thy offerings, and accept thy burnt sacrifice; Selah.

Grant thee according to thine own heart, and fulfil all thy counsel.

We will rejoice in thy salvation, and in the name of our God we will set up our banners: the LORD fulfil all thy petitions.

Now know I that the LORD saveth his anointed; he will hear him from his holy heaven with the saving strength of his right hand.

Some trust in chariots, and some in horses: but we will remember the name of the LORD our God.

They are brought down and fallen: but we are risen, and stand upright.

Save, LORD: let the king hear us when we call.

2 Corinthians: 9:8: And God is able to make all grace abound toward you; that ye, always having all sufficiency in all things, may abound to every good work:

Powerful Prayer Declaration:

The seat of honor meant for me will not be occupied by another. I will always be present on the day of God's visitation in JESUS Name.

The Lord bless me in every area I sought for a change, I am a winner, for God is my victory, I am a Champion. I hold my peace, and God fights my battles; He is my glory and the lifter of my head. God's purpose for me will surely come to pass.

I will keep the faith and testify to His Glory as He perfects all that concerns me in JESUS Name. My life is founded on Christ my Savior, and in Him, I dwell in safety and security.

I am victorious, my life radiates God's glory, and the light of His presence blazes through every representation of darkness. I walk in the light, not in frustration, and I am settled in life because God has blessed me with all things that pertain to life and godliness in CHRIST JESUS Amen.

Prayer points for the Day

- ➤ Sing songs of praise to the Mighty God in Battle.
- ➤ Ask for mercy for every sin committed knowingly and unknowingly.

- By the power in the Name of Jesus, I come against the activities of Satan and his cohorts over my job and the works of my hands.
- By the power in the name of Jesus, I come against every power planning to wreak havoc in my family.
- Every arrow of failure tormenting my works, die, by fire in the name of Jesus.

DAY THIRTY

Scriptural Meditations:

Numbers: 6:24: The LORD bless thee, and keep thee:

The LORD make his face shine upon thee, and be gracious unto thee:

The LORD lift up his countenance upon thee, and give thee peace.

And they shall put my name upon the children of Israel; and I will bless them.

Philippians: 4:13: I can do all things through Christ which strengtheneth me.

Powerful Prayer Declaration:

God is my shield, defense, and tower of strength; I will not see shame and disgrace. Good things will happen for me; the best life comes my way;

because I am destined for the top in JESUS Name Amen.

My faith confessions of divine success come to pass because my words are anointed to produce results. There is no situation I cannot change, for my faith is the victory that overcomes every adversity. Irrespective of what I hear, see or feel, my faith in God's Word prevails. I walk in health, victory, prosperity, and success today, in Jesus' Name.

I am victorious, my life radiates God's glory, and the light of His presence blazes through every representation of darkness. I walk in the light, not in frustration, and I am settled in life because God has blessed me with all things that pertain to life and godliness in CHRIST JESUS.

Good things happen to me because the lines fall for me in pleasant places God loves you perfectly, so I am safe in His hands in JESUS Name Amen.

God is turning my dry ground into pool of water and giving me freshness and a new beginning in JESUS Name Amen.

God has promised to hide me under the shadow of His wings, so I am safe from all storms of life. He whose power never fails shall make a way of escape for me. I am coming out victoriously in JESUS Name Amen.

Prayer Points for the Day

- Prayer of Thanksgiving.
- Prayer of Forgiveness.
- Every spirit of impotency hindering me from rising to the top, Oh God, destroy them by fire. John chapter 5

- ➢ Every arrow attacking my success in my life, My Father, consume them by Fire.
- ➢ Every spirit of confusion manipulating and slowing down my progress in life, I am not your candidate, die by fire.

DAY THIRTY-ONE

Scriptural Meditations:

Luke: 1:48: For he hath regarded the low estate of his handmaiden: for, behold, from henceforth all generations shall call me blessed.

Genesis: 12:2: And I will make of thee a great nation, and I will bless thee, and make thy name great; and thou shalt be a blessing:

Powerful Prayer Declaration:

I have life abundant and life eternal; I have the life of CHRIST flowing in me, so I live and shall not die in JESUS Name.

The glory of God evolves over my life. He lifts me to where He has determined for me from before the foundations of the world. He is good to me, I have found favor, and things are working out for me in JESUS Name.

God is with me; I am a candidate of His eternal glory, and I have joy everlasting.

My hope is eternal. I am guarded with the Spirit of might in my inward man, and I can do all things through CHRIST, who strengthens me in JESUS Name Amen.

The Shout of joy shall not depart from my habitation. God's praise shall continually be in my mouth. And I abound in all that pertains to life and godliness in JESUS Name Amen.

The Lord will answer me in the day of trouble; the name of the God of Jacob set me up on high, and defend me. Send me help from the sanctuary and support, refresh, and strengthen me. May He remember all my offerings and accept my burnt sacrifice. May He grant you according to your heart's desire and fulfill all your plans.

The counsel of God over my life stands sure, He's committed to me, the power of His will sets me in place, and nothing can displace me in JESUS Name.

I have a glorious future; I am created for a purpose. My life is established in the fullness of God's great destiny set ahead of me in JESUS Name Amen.

Prayer points for the Day

- ➢ Sing praise to the Almighty God.
- ➢ Ask for Mercy.
- ➢ Father, let my story change for good and give me a new song in Jesus mighty name.
- ➢ Lord, when others are counting their blessings I will not count my fingers and I shall continue sowing and reaping good fruits in the mighty name of Jesus.

- ➢ Oh Lord, specially attend to my situations today in the mighty name of Jesus.

Powerful Daily Confessions

Isaiah 43:2 KJV

"When thou passest through the waters, I will be with thee; and through the rivers, they shall not overflow thee: when thou walkest through the fire, thou shalt not be burned; neither shall the flame kindle upon thee."

Ezekiel 37:4, 10 KJV

"Again he said unto me, Prophesy upon these bones, and say unto them, O ye dry bones, hear the word of the Lord. So I prophesied as he commanded me, and the breath came into them, and they lived, and stood up upon their feet, an exceeding great army."

'Challenges will come, but those that align with God shall remain Champions'.

Upon the authority of the Word of God, and because I shall walk in the covenant of the Word, I shall not be a victim of the vicissitudes, Waters of depression shall not overwhelm me; Fire of oppression shall not burn me; God's divine presence shall be with me and accompany me everywhere, And I shall come out victorious from all of life's threatening elements, In Jesus' name.

The Power in the Word is in the Authority of the Author of the Word.

Upon the authority of the Word of God,

I speak this morning that,

Every dry bone,

Every hopeless case,

Every dead circumstance,

Every great but buried destiny,

Around and about me now, hear the Word of the LORD and receive life; those situations shall rise as an exceeding mighty army to fulfill the purpose of God to the Glory of God. And I shall surely testify, in Jesus' name.

As the year progresses, my life will not remain stagnant. The precious gift God has in store for me and my household will not elude us. I pray that I will be honored by God this day with the kind of honor no one has ever received in my lineage. I will become a positive reference point to the glory of God in Jesus name. I pray that God will listen to my petitions this year; He will remember me for good. God will cause men who had long forgotten me to remember me and give back to me good things they have denied me. Everyone destined to aid my elevation shall hastily call for me. My mouth will be filled with laughter, Instead of shame and disgrace in my life, business, career, and ministry, God will clothe me with glory and honor.

God will position me in the right place where my divine allocation will meet me. Those who are mocking me and my family in the past will gather and invite others to rejoice with me in the name of Jesus Christ.

This day, through the exceeding great love of God our Savior, I decree that I am entering into an experience of GREAT ABUNDANCE this year.

From today, in all matters of wisdom, grace, health, peace, anointing, favor, and joy, I and all that is mine shall experience "GREAT ABUNDANCE"

I shall come out victorious over every pandemic, virus, an evil wind, demonic conspiracy, and adverse circumstance that will come across my way; and my life shall glorify God, in Jesus' name.

AMEN.

Contact Us

For further spiritual help, please contact the author below

E-mail: ogidanoluwatosin@gmail.com

Other Books by the Author

Eliminate stagnation in your life: 400 prayers that deals with spirit of stagnation

900 Prayers That Break Curses And Spell: Pray Your Way To Supernatural Breakthrough, Blessings And Success: 7 Days Devotions That Break Causes And Spell 21 Days Devotions That Release Favor

Power for Supernatural Breakthrough and Financial Upliftment: 1100 Prayers that Guarantee Success and Great Achievement in your Endeavors: 40 Days Devotions that Releases Miracles, Blessings

Overcoming the Spirit of Difficulties and Struggles: Powerful prayers that breaks the yoke of struggle and difficulties and launches you into uncommon blessings and fulfillment of destiny

Prayers for my Wife: Powerful prayers to change my Wife for better

700 Prayers that Overcome the Spirit of Delayed Breakthrough

You stand a chance to get one free book as a gift; all you need to do is send me a mail telling me how this book has been a blessing to you.